12 WAYS TO SALVAGE your SELF LOVE

BREJETTE TERRY-EMERY

Copyright © 2022 by Brejette Terry-Emery

All rights reserved. No part of this book may be reproduced, stored, or transmitted by any means - whether auditory, graphic, mechanical, or electronic - without written permission of both publisher and author, except in the case of brief excerpts used in critical articles and certain other noncommercial uses permitted by copyright law. Unauthorized reproduction of any part of this work is illegal and is punishable by law.

Unless otherwise noted, scripture quotations are taken from the Holy Bible, New Living Translation, copyright ©1996, 2004, 2015 by Tyndale House Foundation. Used by permission of Tyndale House Publishers, Carol Stream, Illinois 60188. All rights reserved.

ISBN 978-0-578-28447-7

Printed and bound in the United States of America

Book Designed by Brand It Beautifully™
www.branditbeautifully.com
allison@imallisondenise.com

DEDICATION

I dedicate this book to all individuals that have lived their lives for everyone else, not realizing the main goal of life is to find and be our best self. When we realize that we matter – our decisions, our thoughts, and our ideas matter – we then have something to offer the world. The mold was broken when you were created; no one else can ever be you because you were uniquely and wonderfully made, flaws and all.

CONTENTS

Acknowledgements. vi

Introduction vii

Chapter One: Identifying Your Need to
    Find Self-Love 1

Chapter Two: What Self-Love is and
    What it is Not 7

Chapter Three: Choose You! 13

Chapter Four: Identify Positive Resources . . . 23

Chapter Five: Mindset 31

Chapter Six: Plan for the Future. 39

Chapter Seven: Figuring Out Where
    You Fit 45

Chapter Eight: Putting it All Together 53

Chapter Nine: I am Here on Purpose 61

Chapter Ten: Fall in Love with Yourself. 69

Chapter Eleven: This is Me 77

Chapter Twelve: Now You Know. 85

About The Author 91

ACKNOWLEDGEMENTS

I WOULD LIKE to thank my tribe. All of you that continue to push me, guide me, support me, and encourage me to be my best self. Thank you, Allison Denise, CEO of Brand It Beautifully™, for your faith and obedience as well as your amazing work and skill. I would like to thank my mom for all of her support and being my number one fan, even when the vision didn't always look clear. Most importantly, I would like to thank my not-so-little miracle, my son K3, for riding this life out with me without complaining. K3, you are what I do all of this for. One day we'll look back and it will all make sense. The long days and nights, the hard times, and the times you might have felt left out. Remember that prayer, faith, and hard work pays off: Mommy is living proof. I love you all and appreciate you more than words could ever express.

INTRODUCTION

HAVE YOU EVER found yourself so lost and in the depths of your pain that you couldn't imagine there ever being an out? Have you ever wondered "is this my reality?" and "is this my forever?" In this book I am going to cover the steps to discovering self-love, what to do with it, and how to carry it with you from now on.

What are your thoughts about self-love? Do you know what self-love is? What are misconceptions of self-love? Have you been loving yourself and putting yourself first? Do you know what you enjoy doing in life and why? If you are unsure of any of these questions but want to find out, you are in the right place. We are going to discuss these points and more as well as take this journey to a continuous life of self-love, together. In each chapter I will share an experience with you or scenario and talk about the tools I utilized in my journey to self-love. Next you will have an activity to complete to exercise the idea in your life. Then you will journal to process. At the end of each chapter, you will be provided an affirmation exercise to speak over your stage in the journey. Say it as often as needed until you are ready for the next step. Utilize each chapter at your own individual pace and time frame.

CHAPTER ONE

IDENTIFYING YOUR NEED TO FIND SELF-LOVE

"When things change inside you, things change around you."
– UNKNOWN

I FOUND MYSELF in the closet on a warm July night. The closet is where I often snuck away to find my peace and quiet in a full house. It was cool and calm there. No one could hear me scream, yell, or cry there. I owed nobody anything there and I did not have to answer questions there. On this warm July night filled with disbelief, I was at a loss for words. I had no answers and I could not fix this. I was tired and overwhelmed. I was overweight, overworked, and underpaid. I had no quick fix. Life, as I had known it for the last 11 years, would be forever changed. He was gone and was never coming back. There was no us, there were no music shows and clubs. There was no more extra mom status with the boys that I had raised with everything I had, even when I had nothing to give. There were no more 'I love you's' or 'I got you's'. There was just me, my mini, and my mom. What now? As I sat there in the cold space that had a scent of clothes and the stench of feet from the many pairs of shoes that surrounded me, I knew this was it. It was over. A pain that I had never felt overcame my body and I began to see straight black. It was then, "this is it." I didn't want to face the questions, the judgment. And I definitely didn't want anyone to feel sorry for me. I had made these decisions to stay over and over and over and so I deserved everything that I was getting... Or did I? I remember telling myself "I cannot take this." As I contemplated just how I was going to end it all, I felt a tiny hand on my shoulder. My little miracle, my smart, yellow-complected son, did he understand? He also seemed filled with disbelief; his head hung low. He stared me in the eyes and said, "Mom, what are we going to do now?" It was then that it clicked. It was no longer just about me.

I had to think about us. If I followed through with this, there was no way that I was going to take him with me. How much pain would that leave him with? There was no way I could get him out of the room. It was then that I decided that I was going to live. I was going to choose me! I was no longer going to give anyone the power to make me feel this low ever again. It was then that my journey to self-love started.

Take a moment to think about a time that you also had to make the decision to choose you. Reflect on a situation that had you feeling similarly like you didn't have the answers you needed to go on. Or maybe this is you now. Are you feeling lost and hopeless? Are you tired of being tired and pulled down by life's circumstances and situations? Oftentimes in life, we have to be our own cheerleaders. I know it's easier said than done, but we can develop tools to help us when we're not able to do it for ourselves. Ways that do not involve chasing others or being at their mercy. Can you commit to you? To make it for you? Not him, her, or them, but you!? Answer these questions below.

IN THIS ACTIVITY, let's just start by releasing your thoughts on self-love and what you plan to receive from this journey on the lines provided below.

_____

_____

_____

_____

_____

_____

_____

_____

_____

_____

_____

_____

NOW I NEED you to think for a moment: are you ready for change? Are you ready to free your mind of the heavy burdens of feeling less than, not good enough, or all on your own? Are you currently looking for others to validate your existence and lift you up? Write out your thoughts and feelings. Free your mind.

_____

_____

_____

_____

_____

_____

_____

_____

_____

_____

Please take a moment to say this out loud. Say it in the moments that you need the most support. A good time might be early in the morning when you first wake up, in the middle of the day when you are losing momentum, or right before bed to clear your mind. Or you can use it in all the above but state this affirmation to yourself each day until you are ready to move to the next step.

Affirmation

I am committed to starting this journey of self-love and I am going to commit to having an open mind. I am open to being positive and searching within to love myself as I am and with all of me. I am perfectly me. There is only one me. Compare myself to who? I strive to be a better me today than I was the day before.

CHAPTER TWO

WHAT SELF-LOVE IS AND WHAT IT IS NOT

"My self-worth is not determined by others."
– UNKNOWN

BEFORE WE CAN discover self-love, we have to understand: what is self-love? Self-love means having a high regard for your own well-being and happiness.

> *Self-love means taking care of your own needs and not sacrificing your well-being to please others. Figuring out what self-love looks like for you as an individual is an important part of your mental health.* Feb 12,

2020, Self-Love and What It Means | Brain & Behavior Research, www.bbrfoundation.org > blog > self-love-and-what-it-is

I was guilty of always putting everyone and everything before myself, regardless of my needs or how I felt. I would often go without buying myself the basics, like socks and underwear, and had lost the desire to shop for myself because I felt that what everyone else needed was much more important. It is important to switch out your undergarments and to buy yourself new socks when the old ones get raggedy, but when you are caught up in everyone else, you lose sight of the importance of taking care of yourself. I remember taking time off for the kids' appointments and sports but would fall behind on my check-ups, doctor's appointments, and preventive care. This meant that when I was sick, it was very severe. I would have to go to the hospital and be forced to take multiple days off because I wasn't taking care of myself on a daily basis. This also led to major toothaches because I wasn't getting the preventive work taken care of. I'm sure you get my drift, but when we do not take care of the small things, like listening to our body when we need rest or failing to get ahead of the situation, it leads to worse things that might take more time for what was once a quick fix.

There are many ideas of self-love and perceptions of what it is and what it isn't. The misconceptions of self-love include the point that self-love is often perceived as selfish or as a narcissist characteristic. Self-love is not saying that others aren't important and that you are the only one that is important. Rather, it is stating that you are most important in your life – or at least you should be. It is stating that you cannot love anyone else until you learn to love yourself, because otherwise what are you measuring love against? The way that others loved you? A mother's love for a child is just that. A spouse's love for a spouse is just that. But love cannot be cross-measured. Self-love is most important because you are the key "*player in your life,*" in the words of Katt Williams. Until you learn to take care of you, look out for you, and enjoy you, you will never get the full effects and intent of love. You will continue to chase others, to look for the definition of love and the feeling of love from others and in things. Therefore, when those things are no longer there, you are stuck back where you started, feeling empty and unloved.

ANSWER THESE QUESTIONS. Are you someone that has believed the misconceptions of self-love? If so, what were they? Why do you feel that you believed these to be true? Are you open to allowing your mind to be free of those misconceptions?

_____

_____

_____

_____

_____

_____

_____

_____

_____

_____

_____

Please take a moment to say this out loud. You can include this with the previous affirmation or in place of it until you are ready for the next step.

Affirmation

I have been guilty of not understanding the need for self-love and believing the many misconceptions of self-love. I will no longer be a prisoner to giving everything to everyone else and not giving to me first. I will allow myself the space, time, and energy to love and to understand me.

CHAPTER THREE

CHOOSE YOU!

"You are enough just as you are."
– MEGHAN MARKLE

CHOOSING YOU CAN be confusing and hard. It can be hard to know what the right way is and when the right time is to choose yourself. As mentioned in the misconceptions of self-love, you do not want to be seen as selfish or uncaring for anyone else's feelings. It comes down to if the decision between yourself and others has to do with you feeling uncomfortable or being unsafe. If you are going to have to go without so others can have, that is a good time to choose you.

There were many times that I would give all of myself to the point of depression, anxiety, and/or severe exhaustion. I would never say no because I was worried about what others would think or feel. The harsh reality was that I would give and give and give but when it was my time of need, there was hardly ever anyone willing or able to give to me. They either didn't have it or didn't want to put themselves out. How convenient, huh? We'll give someone our last with expectations for others to do the same and then be mad when they choose themselves. Hello, wake-up call! Something had to give and I had to change that pattern.

In the scenario I shared in the beginning chapter, I shared that, in that moment, I decided that I was going to live. I was going to choose me. In self-love, you have to make a conscious decision that, in every situation, instance, and way, you are going to consciously check-in and recognize how this is making you feel. How is this going to make me feel? Does this feel right? Self-love means understanding that you are important. Everything that you feel is valid and relevant. It is okay to not be okay with everything and to go along with everything just because. If something doesn't feel right, look right, or seem right, it probably isn't right! You have every reason to check in with yourself and to evaluate your feelings in that situation. In choosing yourself, you have to understand who you are. Who are you? What has molded the person that you are? The good? The bad? The right? The wrong? Who are you? I remember, after being separated and then divorced, someone once asked me "What do you like to do?" That seems simple, right? But I really had no idea. I was so used to being caught up in everyone else's agenda, life, and needs that I didn't even know what I liked to do. It took me a couple of months to think about and be able to genuinely answer that question.

Activity

START WITH THE easy answers and the superficial, then dig deeper. It might be a little depressing or sad now but, as we take this journey, it will get easier. Use the sheet to jot down who you are. This is a no-judgment zone. Be free to list what you need to list. Some may be able to go as deep as "I am an addict." Some may have a huge list and some might only have three things, but that's okay. You can come back each day that you think of something new and add to what and who you are as you start to discover yourself. Example: I am a daughter, a mother, African American, I am sensitive, I can be moody, I am abandoned, I am used, I am weak, I am lost, I am sad, I am a product of parents who were loving yet tough. List them out. This is a no-judgment zone. Be free to list what you need to list.

    Who are you?

_____

_____

_____

Activity

NOW TAKE A moment to think about things that you actually like to do. We all have busy lives and can't always do everything that we want to, but, if you had a moment and resources were unlimited, what would you do? Again, start simple. Do you like to be inside or outside? Why or why not? Do you like walks in the park? Do you like to take showers for relaxation or baths? Do you like crowds? Do you like to shop? Start to create your own list and continue to write why and why not. With everything that you list, you will develop more and more about yourself. You will discover if you are a people person, also known as an extrovert. Do you like crowded places or quiet places? Etc. This will all help you to discover more about who you are. You will understand more and more about why you are how you are and be able to accept that, rather than it being good, bad, right, or wrong, at this point, it is simply who you are and that is okay.

What do you like to do?

NOW THAT YOU have created your list, I want you to take a moment to journal what you listed out. Did you discover something new that you didn't know about yourself? What did you like the most about your list? What did you like the least about your list?

_____

_____

_____

_____

_____

_____

_____

_____

_____

_____

TAKE SOME TIME to journal about your thoughts for a release before you go to bed tonight or start your day. (Remember, there's no rush with these activities and you can always come back later to add.)

_____

_____

_____

_____

_____

_____

_____

_____

_____

_____

_____

Please take a moment to say this out loud. You can include this with the previous affirmation or in place of it until you are ready for the next step.

Affirmation

Today I choose me. I choose to accept who I am and what I am today. I will not worry about changes at this point because right now, in this very moment, I am me. I will make a conscious decision to learn me and love me more and more each day. I choose to take time to process how things make me feel and why. I will self-check when I feel like something is wrong. I will not just go with the flow without evaluating what I want and need in each situation, because I am important and so are my needs and wants. Today I choose me.

CHAPTER FOUR

IDENTIFY POSITIVE RESOURCES

"If you do not like the road you're walking, start paving another one."
– DOLLY PARTON

AFTER I DECIDED to choose me, I had to figure out my part in the unhappiness in my life. I was overweight, I was depressed, I had crazy anxiety, and I had to figure out where to go from here. I had to ask myself, "How did I get here?" This space I was in, mentally and physically, was somewhere I had been for a very long time. The people-pleasing, always worrying about what everyone thought, and taking everything stated to me to heart. I was hypersensitive to things that didn't matter, such as others' thoughts, needs, wants, and perceptions of me and my life. And then I wasn't taking things that mattered seriously, such as my mental and physical health and my wants and needs. So now… What was I going to do? I was going to take one second at a time until I could get to the minute, then from the minute to the hour. The hour to the day, the day to the week. I would take it month by month until they added up to years, but I knew it was time to find my happiness for me. I started my journey by taking to social media. Instead of giving everyone the negative and victimized play by play on my situation, I was going to block all negative energy and do everything I could to protect my feelings and my side of the story. Instead of being the victim in the situation, I was going to post what I needed to hear each day. I would post things such as "you got this girl!" "No need to fear, this is only the start to a new beginning." "You are a queen so pick up that crown." I started to search for things to motivate me and lift my spirits: positive posts and sites. I would then print them and put them all over my office. During this hard time, I reached out to my boss to see if I could work from home and I was told that wasn't an option. I was now a single mom and I didn't have much PTO, so I had to woman up – in the words of one of my sisters – and take this day by day. So, I took a day or two off and used that time to get myself together. I cried, I yelled, I wrote, and I reached out to family and friends, but even in that, there was only so much they knew and could do. In that moment, I continued to encourage myself and to tell myself the things I thought I needed to hear from others. At this time, I was often sitting in my room alone. I was very sad and hurt. I felt betrayed and alone. I felt lost. I was often in the dark or in a faint light, sitting on my bed. I was in the state of New Mexico, I was employed, and I was enduring, although it was hard.

IN THIS ASSIGNMENT I want you to take a moment to think about where you are. Physically, mentally, emotionally, where are you? Take some time to think literally, physically, and emotionally. Where are you right now? List it out as detailed as you would like.

_____

_____

_____

_____

_____

_____

_____

_____

_____

_____

NOW THAT YOU'VE done that, take a moment to think about where you would like to be. Then, is it as soon as tomorrow or a year from now? Ten years from now? Where would you like to be?

_____

_____

_____

_____

_____

_____

_____

_____

_____

_____

TAKE A MOMENT to process and journal all that you have written. Did any of these thoughts surprise you? If so, why? Did you like the thoughts that came out? Why or why not? Again, if you don't have all the answers now, you can always come back and add to your list or journal.

_____

_____

_____

_____

_____

_____

_____

_____

_____

_____

Read this out loud. Include it with your previous affirmations or put it in place of them until you are ready for the next step.

Affirmation

Now that I have chosen me continuously, I am also choosing to search for things in my life that bring me peace. I will no longer associate myself with the drama of my past or my situation. I will block out or choose to not engage in conversations or situations that make me anxious or that make me want to climb back into that sad place.

I will look for quotes, posts, and groups that lift me up. I deserve to be happy and I am going to continue to strive each day to find something that makes me happy or grateful. I deserve my heart's desires and I will work to gain them within and for myself.

CHAPTER FIVE

MINDSET

"A fresh start isn't a new place, it's a new mindset."
– UNKNOWN

SO, ON THIS journey, I went back to work after a couple of days – and I'm not going to lie, it was so hard. Due to certain mutual people and acquaintances, word was getting out fast about the drastic change that had taken place. So, then there came the questions and comments in person, by text, by call, and by social media. Everyone wanted updates and wanted to give me updates on what was taking place on the other end. I found myself questioning when I would ever get through this. I would sit at my desk and cry or try to run to the bathroom before anyone could catch me when the memories of what was and what would no longer be would fill my mind. The laughs, the fun times, everything that I had known. I found it hard to eat and wanted to spend time with others less and less. The hurt, the pain, and even the betrayal... But I had other obligations that I couldn't fail. In the midst of the chaos, I had started to plan my business with my team and I had to show up. I decided to let everyone know that if they weren't for me and didn't mean me well, then to leave me alone as the situation was hard enough. I would shut people down when they would ask questions and I wouldn't answer my phone if individuals weren't in my immediate circle. I would look for motivational speakers and sermons to help me through the days and sleepless nights. When my eyes would be so heavy that even closing them would hurt, when tears would flow without me even noticing until my pillow was soaked, I would listen to individuals like T. D. Jakes, Michael Todd, Steven Furtick. I followed Trenton Shelton on all social media platforms. These were individuals that often spoke to my pain and my soul. They helped give me vision of the other side of my pain and helped me to see some light in my situation. This was my way of changing my mindset and how I saw my life and the different situations I had gone through. For everything I saw as negative, I learned big lessons. In everything I put up with that I did not want to, I learned to no longer do that. I learned what kind of relationship or partner traits I did not want. I learned what made me sad and became angry that I had put up with so much yet demanded so little in return. But that was my choice, so I could not be mad at anyone but myself. I could not control my past, but I could most certainly choose how I was going to move forward.

We have to understand that life is what we make of it. If we think and expect bad, that is exactly what is going to continue to come. But if we take time to analyze and extract the lessons learned and the positives in each situation, our outcome will be a lot lighter. We will be able to find peace in the situations that we face. At times, it's bigger than something we can control, and we have to find additional support, such as a counselor or therapist. For those that have passed through the trauma in their life, a life coach is a good option for help in continuing to plan for the future and to attain those future goals.

IN THIS ASSIGNMENT I want you to think answer: what are some things you've always wanted to do? What places have you always wanted to visit or loved visiting? What things might you have enjoyed as a child or adolescent, when life was a little less demanding? List these thoughts out. Don't worry about how you would get there or the cost; dare to daydream.

_____

_____

_____

_____

_____

_____

_____

_____

PROCESS THOSE PLACES and think about how you felt there. What did you like about those places? Be as descriptive as you can be.

_____

_____

_____

_____

_____

_____

_____

_____

_____

_____

_____

_____

STEP FURTHER. I'M tasking you with researching and finding a public figure that you can relate to or that you might be able to connect with. If you're a reader, find a book that speaks to your situation. If you're a person that needs dialogue, search for motivational speakers on YouTube or other social media sites. You can look into those that come up by popular demand but keep searching until you find material that speaks to your pain. List them below. Everyone is not for everyone so find a few that work for you.

_____

_____

_____

_____

_____

_____

_____

_____

Read this out loud. Include it with your previous affirmations or put it in place of them until you are ready for the next step.

Affirmation

Not only am I making a conscious effort to choose me, but I am also choosing to find peace and joy. I am going to choose to be intentional. I am going to choose to find happiness instead of sadness. I am going to choose to find something positive in every negative thing that I encounter in my life. I am going to choose to have a positive mindset and to find the glass half full when my mind wants me to see it as half empty.

CHAPTER SIX

PLAN FOR THE FUTURE

"If you want something you've never had, you must be willing to do something you've never done."
– THOMAS JEFFERSON

AS TIME WENT on, the days got easier. As I started being conscious of the energy and vibes I allowed in my space, life seemed less heavy and more enjoyable. I removed myself from others that were drama-fueled and always full of gossip. I even changed the amount of television I was consuming and when I watched the type of things I watched. I couldn't stand certain television genres because they made me sick. The public humiliation and fun that it made of very real situations and others' pain were unbearable to me. So, I stopped watching it and started watching things that helped me feel good, to want to continue to do good for others. For the first time in my life, I was able to think just for me and my mini, not a whole house full. I was still pretty busy getting the business plan underway and completing forms and such with my team, but I enjoyed the process. I filled my time with things that mattered, meaning I therefore had less time to give to things that didn't. I was less sad because I had less time to cry. I was less depressed because I had positive things to look forward to. At this time, I was feeling free to spend time with my circle from time to time. I would catch up with friends that I hadn't in a long time and I was able to get out at night to enjoy the music I liked and the crowds I liked. I was starting to remember what I liked to do and what I didn't like to do. I started to be in the moment and to take in joyful times and laughs instead of trying to cover up my pain with work and everyone else's agendas. I started to take girls' trips and go on weekend getaways. This actually was feeling pretty good.

    When you take time to think and feel, to process and rest, you are able to see things a lot more clearly. You aren't forcing your body or mind into making decisions on the fly or signing yourself up for things you really don't want to do. When your mind is clear, you understand that everything not everything has to be answered then and there. Everything should be processed and thought about before you give your yes. This also means that you can actually think about your future and what that looks like for you. Not everyone and everything else, but what it is that you would truly like to see, conquer, and achieve.

IN THIS ASSIGNMENT, think about some of the goals that have been sitting at the back of your mind for a long time. What are some hobbies that you used to enjoy but stopped due to other obligations? Did you used to sew or draw? Did you used to crochet or weave? Did you used to like to go out dancing or to listen to music at your favorite spot? List these places and things out.

_____

_____

_____

_____

_____

_____

_____

_____

_____

NOW PROCESS WHAT you enjoy about them. How did you feel while doing those things and why? What are some positive memories that you have about those times?

_____

_____

_____

_____

_____

_____

_____

_____

_____

_____

_____

_____

_____

Read this out loud. Include it with your previous affirmations or put it in place of them until you are ready for the next step.

Affirmation

I am going to make time to get back to the things that I used to enjoy. My days are getting a little brighter and my heart is feeling a little lighter. I am not where I want to be but I am working each day to get to a place I would like to be. I am going to continue to take this one day at a time. I choose me not just today but every day! I am going to be happy and I am going to be at peace. I am going to be filled with joy.

CHAPTER SEVEN

FIGURING OUT WHERE YOU FIT

"Purpose: how you use your experiences, talents, and passions to better the lives of those around you"

– L. PETERSON

ONCE I FOUND myself getting on track, I really started to wonder why I was where I was. As I continued to work jobs where I enjoyed the actual work but wasn't feeling the environment or the unrealistic expectations, I started to think there had to be more to life than living to work and working to live. The non-profit was well underway and we had been granted the affiliates for one of our programs. At this time, I was juggling working full-time while running the non-profit part-time on every lunch break and right after work until late hours of the night. I had a conversation with God on where He really wanted me and where my gifts and talents would be seen as more than just pushing numbers. I was then asked to apply for a management position, something I had always wanted as an opportunity to showcase my leadership skills and work ethic. As I interviewed, I soon came to realize that if I were to take the position, it would be more of a battle than a blessing and I would have to let go of all that my team and I had worked so hard for, because I wouldn't have any extra time. It was then that I realized there was a purpose to all that I had experienced and I was going to be used for something new. Something I had never dreamed of and something I had never planned for. I continued to watch the videos and listen to my gospel music and, as I continued to take time with Him and those He sent, He slowly developed it all for me little by little. There were many that would come to join the journey and very little that would stay. These are parts of our journey that are called seasons. The times that we plant. We water and we tend and then we wait... Self-discovery, self-discipline, and self-awareness are very important on this journey because, in order to know where we're going, we have to know who we are and where we come from. We have to think about all the things that have made us who we are. Once we process those different situations and feelings, once we think about the lessons of it all, we see the connections as to how it all adds up to equal YOU. As you have been taking the steps to figure out who you are, where you are, and how you can, you are now tapping into why you are.

Activity

IN THIS ACTIVITY I want you to think about the major situations in your life and look at them from the perspective of what you learned in each of those situations. What did it teach me? What did I take away to use in situations that might be similar, moving forward? What could I have done differently? What worked well? Take time to process your past and present friendships, relationships, careers and/or jobs, and family situations. As all of these things have helped to develop your likes, your dislikes, your attitudes, your aggressiveness, your passiveness, etc.

Why am I?

_____

_____

_____

_____

_____

_____

NOW LET'S SEE what you learned from breaking it all down. What did you take away from breaking this all down? I hope that you understand that there's something to be learned from every situation. Rather, is it in the way that we continue to trust without looking at the warning signs or that we give to a fault? Are you extremely closed off in order to protect your heart, but you often find that you also block those amazing people that are sent to help you grow and to love you? There's good and bad in us all but, regardless of anything, you must learn to accept and love it all. Change what you do not like and really hone into those things that you absolutely love about yourself.

_____

_____

_____

_____

_____

Today I, (say your name), am continuing to choose me. I am choosing to surround myself with things that lift my spirits and help me to grow. I have decided to pick back up or to include _____ into my routine because I enjoy it. I have decided that I enjoy listening to or reading material from _____. I have decided that I will no longer allow people or things into my life that do not add to me. I am choosing to see the lesson in all things that are sent my way – rather they challenge me or make me grow. My goals are now my focus in order to get out of life what I wish to see. I realize that there is purpose to my pain and I am striving each day to be the best me I can possibly be.

CHAPTER EIGHT

PUTTING IT ALL TOGETHER

"Difficult roads often lead to beautiful destinations."
– ZIG ZIGLAR

I HAD CHOSEN not to take the job opportunity after weighing my pros and cons, but would soon face a lay off. After some long talks with my mentors and God, I was led to take the walk of faith and to run the non-profit full-time. Now, this was way harder than anything I could have ever imagined. I had been on my own since the age of 17 and I was raised to always have my own. This led to me learning how and when to ask for help. Ask for help? You mean I have to let everyone know that, for once in my life, I was admitting that I didn't have it all together? I went into this without any major funding in the non-profit, no side hustle or job in the running – just me, God, and all the numerous individuals He would send my way to build the dream. So I went on this journey knowing that by the time my unemployment went out, something was going to come through. Well, the six months came and went and no funding came in. I kept asking God should I be applying for jobs, or…? Every time that I would ask, I would get down to dollars and change and there would come some type of contract work or a side job to get me through until the next season. I soon found myself leaning on what I was good at. I was good at lifting others up and supporting their dreams and goals. I was always the go-to any time others were down or just needing a helping hand. With my background in school and career, I was led to inspiration and empowerment coaching and speaking. I was led to become a coauthor and later an author. I used all the hurts, pains, abandonment, and hard times to relate to others' pain and hardships when I was working with them. I took all those things that were sent to break me and used them to lift others – and, in lifting others, I learned to lift myself.

Activity

When will I? You've probably come to this part of the book and are like, "well, now what?" It's time to start applying these principles to your daily life. Change is a mindset and all about being conscious about the way things make you feel and why. It's important to know who you are so that you also know who you are not. It is important for you to have standards and expectations because, paraphrasing, the one that stands for nothing will fall for anything – Zig Zigler. Everything and everyone that comes into your life should be pouring into you and vice versa. Anyone or thing that is not pouring in is definitely taking. Any time that energy is being given, something has to replace its space or it will remain empty. No one can pour from an empty cup. Try it.

Go to your cabinet and take a cup out. Now turn it over onto the counter and see what happens. Absolutely nothing. When you take a cup full of water and pour it out into the sink, the liquid is now transferred. What's left in the cup? Nothing. But if you take a pitcher and fill it to the top, then take down some cups and pour the liquid into those cups, you will notice you have enough for several cups or another large container. Think of that liquid as your happiness and your peace. Your joy. Just as hard of a battle as it is to get there, you have to work hard to stay there. That means you have to practice continuously. It gets easier and then it becomes your new norm. You will notice that you won't tolerate just anything. You will put more thought into things before you give that yes. You will learn that 'no' will become a regular part of your vocabulary and you will start doing the things that you enjoy. It's perfectly fine to try new things, that isn't what this is saying. Equally, you might give every once in a while. The point is that you will be more reluctant to interrupt your peace, joy, and happiness.

TAKE SOME TIME to look at your strengths today. What are some things that you do really well? What skills do you naturally possess? Are you a good cook or baker? Are you creative in terms of drawing or singing? Look into those things you listed that you enjoyed doing and why. Are you good at working with others? Do you naturally like to work solo? There are no right or wrong answers. Your truth is your truth.

_____

_____

_____

_____

_____

_____

_____

_____

DID ANYTHING ABOUT this list shock you? Were there things that you forgot you were really good at? How can you incorporate these things as part of your daily routine?

_____

_____

_____

_____

_____

_____

_____

_____

_____

_____

_____

_____

_____

Affirmation

From this day forward, I am going to focus on why I am. I understand that I am still here through it all; I am still here. I am going to home in on what I do well and use that to manifest my purpose. I am going to continue to incorporate things that I do well into my life. I am going to choose to add things into my life that help me feel good about myself, where I am today, and where I envision myself to be in 5 to 10 years from now. I have purpose and I am here on purpose.

CHAPTER NINE

I AM HERE ON PURPOSE

"Find a purpose in life so big it will challenge every capacity to be at your best."
– UNKNOWN

WE ARE ALL special in our own way. We have amazing talents and gifts that we never really had to work hard for and that came naturally. Yes, we might have to put this skill back in play or dust the instrument off and have it tuned up, but there are certain things that we have no matter what. No one can take them away from us, as they were not given to us by anybody... At this point, we have to live intentionally. Do everything with intention or for a reason. Every decision you make affects you in some way. Live every day to get something out of it. Turn every rough day into a learning experience. I was running out of the house in a rush and spilled coffee all over my new outfit and my kitchen. What could I have done differently? Taken some time to slow down. Given myself more time in the mornings. Maybe I'm being slowed down so I miss that car accident or to allow me to pick up that call that's coming in from someone that might have needed me in that very moment. See, when we look at things with an open mind and without making everything about us (selfishly, but in a loving, free will way), we are able to process our meaning in this thing called life. Understand that many did not make it to this day and would give anything to have the opportunity to spill coffee, if that meant they were able to get another day with their kid or their spouse. We often take the facts and make them negative by default. We are programmed in this world to take every situation and to focus on the negatives. However, there is something positive every day. Someone didn't get to achieve the dreams they had once they set forth, nor even the opportunity to get another day to try – but you are still here. You're not just here because you're owed another day. No day is promised to any of us. So, being that you are here, what are you planning to do with this time? Time is going to pass regardless of what you're doing or what is going on around you. Hardships are going to come, people that we love are going to pass, friends are going to come and go, and love may not always be on our side, but what are you going to do for you? We cannot control any of these situations, but we can control what we can do now. We often take for granted that for every breath we breathe, someone could be losing theirs. A mother has lost a child, a child has lost a parent, a sister has lost their sibling, but you have some of yours still around. Live in the moment. Take it all in and learn to appreciate everything that you still are able to do, see, and the moments you are able to live.

Activity

I WANT YOU to remember that you are here on purpose – and that means there is a reason for you still being here. What are you doing with that time? What are you supposed to be building or creating? What are you supposed to be adding to the world? Someone is out there, waiting on you to step up and do what you have always wanted to do. Let's think about this. What can you do today to get closer to the gifts and talents that you listed yesterday? What are some free or low-cost tools that are out there which can support you in leveling up to that next level? What are some classes or workshops that you might be able to sit in on? Take some time to do the research and intentionally build up your tool belt. You may not have everything to go all the way, but *"shoot for the moon, even if you miss, you'll land among the stars" ~ Les Brown*, which means that you can get somewhere close.

_____

_____

_____

LET'S JOURNAL ABOUT what some of those ideas are. What are your thoughts or next steps towards actually signing up for those classes and/ workshops? What are some deadlines that you can give yourself to help motivate this change?

_____

_____

_____

_____

_____

_____

_____

_____

_____

_____

Affirmation

Today I am deciding to take the next steps towards finding out why I am here. I am intentionally seeking resources that will help me get to the next level and I am not believing any of the excuses that I come up with as to why I can't. I can do anything that I put my mind to. Everything is possible as long as I show up each day. I was made for such a time as this!

CHAPTER TEN

FALL IN LOVE WITH YOURSELF

"How you love yourself is how you teach others to love you."
– RUPI KAUR

AS I STARTED to find my way, others wanted to be added to the equation. However, I found myself afraid to let anyone in. I understood at this point that I enjoyed the peace and the joy of life again. So, as I started to think about letting others in, I had to remember that everyone has a motive and I treated everyone as such. Not all motives are bad motives, but a motive is a motive nonetheless. I had to realize that many people come to take. They are drawn to you because you carry a light that everyone wants but which they are not willing to work hard enough to find within themselves. They want your time and attention when it's convenient for them, yet when you're in need they're nowhere to be found. I had to realize that I'd better get used to being alone. We have the misconception that because someone is alone, they are lonely. That's not always the case. Sometimes others are alone because they haven't found anyone worth allowing into their space. Or we understand that we can control our actions and feelings and cannot control others' feelings or actions, so it's safer to keep them at bay. But the more that you love yourself, the more you start to teach others how to love you. You are less likely to just dealing with and taking whatever. You now have standards as to what someone can say to you, how they can say it to you, and when it is appropriate. You start to know what it's like to be treated as someone and not just anyone. This often comes off as being selfish or conceited – and there's definitely a thin line – but there's nothing wrong with having standards and rules. Every establishment, company, and setting has rules and standards. When you care about someone or something, you handle it with care. You do not just throw it anywhere or leave it in the corner if you really like it or care about it, so you should have these same standards and expectations. I always say that if you move in your truth, you cannot go wrong. If you move with good intentions and not wanting to take from anyone or hurt anyone, then you're able to say almost anything. For example, your friends invite you to go to a place that makes you uncomfortable. Maybe you aren't a smoker and that specific place is smoky. Any time you go, you come home with a really bad headache and your house smells like smoke, so you have to deal with that headache all week. If you say to them "I do not want to go because that place gives me a headache," that is your truth. NO, you cannot control how that might make them feel. But if it hurts you to go, then why go? Now if you say "I just don't want to go," that might be seen as you being rude or not wanting to compromise. It leaves a lot of gray areas. It's all about how we look at a situation. What is the message that we want to get out? Your truth is your truth.

EVERY DAY I am challenging you to show up for your best. You may not be able to be everything every day, but every day you can be your best with what you have. Think about ways that you can show up in everything that you do. In what ways do you tend to not give all of yourself to the things you do or the relationships that you have? List them out. No particular order or format, just list out ways that you fall short for yourself. Like for me: I procrastinate really badly, so I find myself constantly in a rush or feeling lost and rushed. I often make simple mistakes that could have been avoided if I had just slowed down. I tend to over-promise and under-deliver, even for myself. I promise myself things and then promise everyone else things and am then left overwhelmed and lost. What are some of these patterns that you tend to fall into?

_____

_____

_____

Activity

LASTLY, I CHALLENGE you, now that you have put all of this work in: I want you to take you out on a date. Put on your best outfit, fix up your hair and make-up (if that applies to you), and take yourself to a place that you've always wanted to go to. Choose a place that's in your budget. It can be as simple as a picnic in the park or a day at the aquarium, or to one of the best restaurants in town. Whatever your heart desires within your budget. Spend time with yourself and your thoughts. Think about how far you've come and where your goals and dreams are going to take you. If it makes it less awkward for you, take your journal so you can have a dialogue with yourself. I want you to talk nothing but positive to yourself, no matter what. Treat yourself as you would want someone to treat you on a date. Have fun with it and don't think too hard. While you're on the date or once you return, write down how that made you feel. What were the best parts? I want you to make this a habit. Once a month, take time out to treat yourself and do the things you enjoy doing so that you never forget. No matter how much your life situation changes, hold yourself accountable to you. Include some pictures from your time spent with yourself.

_____

_____

_____

_____

_____

_____

_____

_____

_____

_____

_____

_____

_____

_____

I love me some me! I am different from anyone else that I have ever met because I am perfectly me. I love spending time with me because _ _____. I make myself laugh by _____. I feel like the most fun part about hanging out with me is _____ _____. I will continue to spend time with me and take care of me because I am the most important person in my life – and if I am not okay, I cannot take care of anyone else. I am enough and I am me! I love me some me!

CHAPTER ELEVEN

THIS IS ME

"I am brave, I am bruised, I am who I'm meant to be, this is me."
– JUSTIN PAUL BENJ PASEK

AS YOU START to discover yourself and find all the parts about yourself that you like and dislike, you are able to say that you really know yourself. As you begin to learn yourself, at this stage you should start to actually figure out that you are pretty darn amazing and very special. This isn't to say that you don't have any flaws or character defects, as we all have things that we can and should be working on daily. My goal each day, as cliché as it sounds, is to be the best me in every day. So, if I'm working on being the best me, that means that I have to work on how I make others feel as well. Am I moving in love, honesty, and in understanding, or am I moving in selfishness, jealousy, and judgment? It's important that we move in this world treating others how we would like to be treated. Each day I have learned to love my freckles, my moles, my scars, my big forehead, and all. Each day I have learned to love my big hair. In learning to love me, I have learned how to take care of myself and how to listen to my body. I have learned to enter each day and each situation with a positive mind and open heart – but also while knowing how I would like to be treated in the same instance. Now that I am aware of what I like and do not like about me and my character, I can identify those things in other people. If I'm in a situation that doesn't make me feel good or add to my positive vibe, I have learned that it is important to exit that conversation or situation respectfully. As we have talked about above, it is important to protect your peace, your joy, and your sanity. It is your job and yours alone. So, if others don't like who you are and what comes with it, they probably shouldn't be in your space or able to feed off your energy. And that's perfectly okay.

We aren't for everybody and not everybody is for us. I get the question a lot: does this go for family as well? Yes, family is included in this as well. If they cannot love you as you are, then they do not need to be in your company or your space. We hear a lot that it is okay to love people from afar and not be bothered with them. Anything that isn't pouring into you is taking from you. All relationships and situations in your life should add to your positive vibe. This isn't to say that every day is going to be perfect, but you definitely have the power to choose how much and to what degree you allow it to affect you. For instance, if you're having an amazing day and it seems that every time you're in a good mood, you get around that one friend, coworker, or acquaintance and your entire attitude and/or mindset changes? That's a sign of someone that you might need to spend less time around or that might not need to be in your space. If, every time you go to your place of employment, you feel sick or you really dislike preparing to go, it\s time for you to start looking for another place of employment. I remember, as mentioned in the opening of this book, that nothing in my life brought me joy and I was always looking for an outlet. Until I took the time to self-discover, I felt I had to take certain things or put up with certain things. However, that isn't true and there are a lot of things about our surroundings that we can change, one being who you surround yourself with. The people you share your private business with. Your place of employment. When God made that company or agency, He made a million more like it. If you aren't happy with your pay, what are some things that you can do about that? You can look into what it would take to move to the next level as a manager or supervisor. Or is it time for a change in the type of career you're in? Is it time to go back to school or to join a certificate program? With all of this said, we have to get to a point in our lives where we're happy with who we are and where we are. Until we get to that point, we have to work every day to get to where we want to be. Each part of our journey is giving us tools, giving us materials, and teaching us lessons that we will need as we get closer to where we need to be.

TAKE SOME TIME to jot down the people, places, or situations that make us feel less than. That make us question our beauty or weight. The things that make us feel insecure or unsure of who we are. List them out.

_____

_____

_____

_____

_____

_____

_____

_____

_____

_____

_____

NOW TAKE SOME time to add some detail as to how we can gradually change what we can control in each of these situations. If it isn't something that you can control, then it might be time to cut something loose. What might those be and what are respectable ways that you can cut those ties?

_____

_____

_____

_____

_____

_____

_____

_____

_____

_____

Affirmation

I am me. Unapologetically, I am me. Every person in my life, from this day forward, will have to take me as I am – with my flaws and all – or leave me. I am working to be a better me in every way and every day. I will continue to show up for me every day. The more I grow, the better the version of me will become. I am in competition with no one but myself. I was made because I am unique and I am beautiful in my own ways, not to be compared with anyone else.

CHAPTER TWELVE

NOW YOU KNOW

"Do the best you can until you know better. Then when you know better, do better."
– MAYA ANGELOU

IN THIS BOOK we have talked about the definition of self-love. We have covered what self-love is not and the misconceptions of self-love. We have talked about how to discover our self-love and received some tools on how to guide the journey.

Love is not to be defined as #couplegoals or superficial social media appearances with a loved one or significant other. Love is defined in those silent moments where you are filled with the soft, brisk tingles of happiness, joy, and peace. These can be created from an electronic bond formed with another but also from within yourself. Love is knowing, in the pit of your heart and within the butterflies of your stomach, that everything is going to be okay. Love is not being filled with questions of 'what if's or tricking your mind with the 'at least'... "What if I could feel wanted?" and "At least they come home, even if it is in the wee hours of the morning." Again, love is peace. The peace of smiling because you are really enjoying life and the comfort of being okay, even if you\re alone or going through hard times. Enjoying your own company and being comfortable with silence may take time but it is necessary. While writing this book, I wondered how to conclude. However, the truth is that self-love is forever a work in progress. In order to have self-love, you have to choose to love you every day, intentionally. You have to take care of yourself before taking care of others. You have to make sure that your basic needs and health are met before you include others into your space. Once you find you and start your self-care journey, take time to go back through these steps every so often so you make sure you never lose yourself or forget you again. Remember that if the love being offered doesn't feel good, isn't intentional, or isn't in sync with your vision or goals, then, no matter how badly you want it, it isn't for you. If it doesn't line up, it's not what's meant for you. This goes for friendships, relationships, work, missions, and visions. If it doesn't help you to feel your absolute best, if you aren't feeling accomplished or amazing, then it is not love. Love makes you feel absolutely amazing – and it is your job to love yourself in every way, every day!

TAKE SOME TIME to reflect on this chapter. In what ways will you work to be intentional in your self-love? How will you work to not leave you out? What was the most important takeaway of this chapter?

_____

_____

_____

_____

_____

_____

_____

_____

_____

_____

_____

NOW LET'S USE the space below to set some goals for your self-love. How often will you revisit self-checking? What activities will stay on your self-care list in managing your self-love?

_____

_____

_____

_____

_____

_____

_____

_____

_____

_____

_____

Affirmation

If the love is real, the love should make me feel absolutely amazing. It will not hurt and it will not cause me to doubt myself or to dislike myself. It is my job to love myself in every way, every day! I choose me intentionally!

ABOUT THE AUTHOR

BREJETTE TERRY-EMERY

BREJETTE N. TERRY-EMERY is a 2x Amazon bestselling author, motivational speaker, inspirational, and empowerment coach. With the many hats that she wears, she is also Co-Founder of the nonprofit Inspirempower New Mexico and Executive Director of its local Dress for Success -Albuquerque, an affiliate of the worldwide Dress for Success organization.

Prior to this role, Brejette served the community and its youth for eight years providing case management, guidance, mentoring, and career pathways for Albuquerque's at-risk youth and their families.

Brejette holds a Bachelor of Science in Family Studies/Human Development and Family Relations, with a minor in Africana Studies from the University of New Mexico. Brejette is passionate about walking in her innate God-given purpose and most importantly raising her amazingly, bright son.

www.ingramcontent.com/pod-product-compliance
Lightning Source LLC
Chambersburg PA
CBHW050655160426
43194CB00010B/1955